DELETE

Epic Cars

Maserati GranTurismo

MEGAN COOLEY PETERSON

BLACK RABBIT BOOKS

Bolt is published by Black Rabbit Books
P.O. Box 3263, Mankato, Minnesota, 56002.
www.blackrabbitbooks.com
Copyright © 2021 Black Rabbit Books

Jen Besel, editor; Grant Gould, designer;
Omay Ayres, photo researcher

Library of Congress Cataloging-in-Publication Data
Names: Peterson, Megan Cooley, author.
Title: Maserati GranTurismo / by Megan Cooley Peterson.
Description: Mankato, Minnesota : Black Rabbit Books, 2021. | Series: Bolt.
  Epic cars | Includes bibliographical references and index. | Audience:
  Ages 8-12. | Audience: Grades 4-6. | Summary: "Experience what it's like
  to be behind the wheel of a Maserati GranTurismo through exciting text,
  vibrant photography, and labeled images and other graphics"— Provided
  by publisher.
Identifiers: LCCN 2019027457 (print) | LCCN 2019027458 (ebook) |
ISBN 9781623102562 (hardcover) | ISBN 9781644663523 (paperback) |
ISBN 9781623103507 (ebook)
Subjects: LCSH: Maserati GranTurismo automobile—Juvenile literature.
Classification: LCC TL215.M34 P48 2021 (print) | LCC TL215.M34 (ebook) |
DDC 629.222/2—dc23
LC record available at https://lccn.loc.gov/2019027457
LC ebook record available at https://lccn.loc.gov/2019027458

Printed in the United States. 4/20

Image Credits

Contents

CHAPTER 1

Racing Down
the Road. 4

CHAPTER 2

Design. 10

CHAPTER 3

Power and
Performance. 20

CHAPTER 4

An Epic Car. 29

Other Resources. 30

Racing
Down the Road

The Maserati GranTurismo looks like a sculpture. But it drives like a race car. This supercar hits 60 miles (97 kilometers) per hour in just 4.8 seconds. Its engine roars as it tears down the road.

EARLY MASERATI
RACE CAR

A6 1500 GT

11922 · SA

6

A Long History

The Maserati company started in 1914. It made race cars. More than 30 years later, Maserati came out with its first GranTurismo. It was called the A6 1500 GT Pininfarina. This car had a racing engine. But it was built for the road.

Maserati only made 61 A6 1500 GTs.

1947

Maserati introduces its first GranTurismo, the A6 1500 GT Pininfarina.

1940 |||||||||||||||||||||||||||||||||||||||||||||

The 3500 GT **debuts**. This was the first GranTurismo made in large numbers.

1957

2007

A redesigned GranTurismo is **unveiled** at the Geneva Motor Show.

2018

An upgraded GranTurismo hits the road.

The GranTurismo MC Stradale debuts at the Paris Motor Show.

2010

2020

CHAPTER 2

Design

The GranTurismo was designed to stand out. The car's smooth body reduces **drag**. Air easily passes over it. The GranTurismo has Maserati's **iconic** triple side vents. Air passes through these vents and cools the engine.

TRIPLE SIDE VENTS

WHEELS

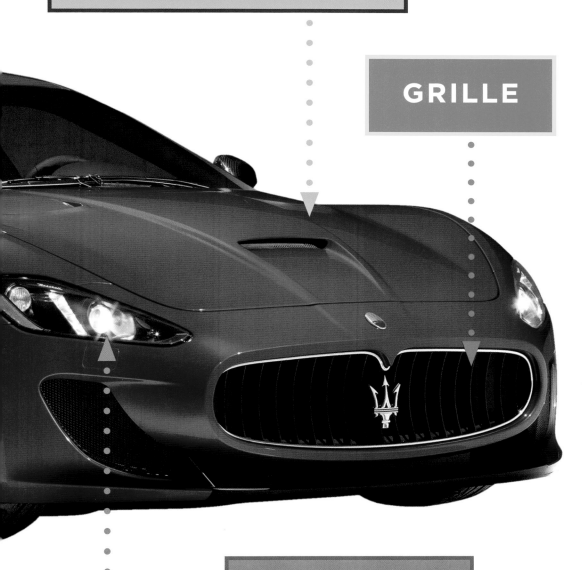

LONG FRONT END

GRILLE

LED HEADLIGHTS

Models

Maserati makes two GranTurismo models today. The Sport is the base model. The MC has a few design upgrades. It has an optional **carbon fiber** hood. The hood also has an air intake and air vents. The air intake gives the engine more power. Air vents create downforce. Downforce keeps the car steady at high speeds.

• ▶

MC stands for Maserati Corsa.

MC

GranTurismo means "grand touring"
in Italian. Touring cars can make long
trips in comfort and style.

Interior

The interior of the GranTurismo is classic and simple. The front seats come in carbon fiber, leather, or fabric. They easily slide forward so passengers can climb into the backseat. Ten speakers bring the car's sound system to life. A touch screen controls the car's music and maps.

Personalized

Buyers can personalize their GranTurismos. They can choose from three different steering wheels. The wheel can be all leather, carbon fiber, or a mix of leather and fabric. The cars come in several exterior and interior color choices.

Design Choices for the GranTurismo

16 EXTERIOR PAINT COLORS

6 DASHBOARD COLOR OPTIONS

8 SEAT COLORS

12 STITCHING COLOR OPTIONS

19

CHAPTER 3

Power and Performance

The GranTurismo doesn't disappoint under the hood. It comes with an eight-cylinder engine. The engine puts out 460 horsepower. The MC model can hit 187 miles (301 km) per hour.

MC

4.7 SECONDS

TIME TO GO FROM **0 to 60 MILES** (97 KM) PER HOUR

2019 GRANTURISMO SPORT VS. MC

SPORT

TOP SPEED
186
MILES
(299 km) per hour

460
horsepower

4.8
SECONDS

TIME TO GO FROM
0 to 60 MILES
(97 KM) PER HOUR

TOP SPEED
187
MILES
(301 km) per hour

460
horsepower

The GranTurismo's engine is built by Ferrari.

Driving Modes

The GranTurismo has a driving mode to fit every driver. Each mode changes the way the car handles. Drivers can choose between automatic and **manual** modes. Sport mode makes the engine crackle. Drivers feel like they're on the race track.

Suspension

The GranTurismo delivers both speed and a comfortable ride. The car has a double-wishbone **suspension**. In this system, each wheel has its own control arms and **shock absorbers**. If one wheel hits a bump, the other wheels aren't affected. This design creates a smoother, tighter ride.

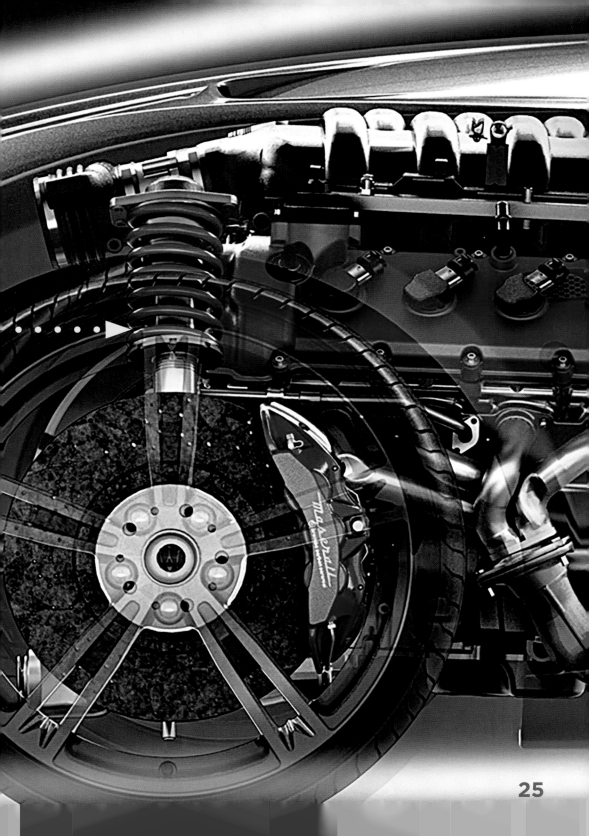

4

TOTAL SEATING

By the Numbers

20
miles (32 km)
per gallon

HIGHWAY GAS MILEAGE

$151,720

BASE PRICE
FOR A 2018 GRANTURISMO MC

$134,300
BASE PRICE FOR A 2018
GRANTURISMO SPORT

CHAPTER 4

An Epic Car

The GranTurismo demands to be noticed. This epic car combines luxury and power. Drivers can ride in comfort while carving up the road at high speeds.

carbon fiber (KAR-buhn FAHY-bur)—a very strong, lightweight material

debut (day-BYOO)—to make a first appearance

drag (DRAYG)—something that makes action or progress slower or more difficult

iconic (i-KON-ik)—widely recognized and well-established

manual (MAN-yoo-uhl)—a transmission controlled by the driver

shock absorber (SHAHK ub-ZORB-ur)—a device connected to a vehicle's wheel in order to reduce the effect of bumps

suspension (suh-SPEN-shuhn)—the system of springs that supports the upper part of a vehicle on the axles

unveil (un-VAYL)—to make public

BOOKS

Geddis, Norm. *Hop Inside the Most Exotic Cars.*
The World of Automobiles. Broomall, PA: Mason
Crest, 2019.

Bodensteiner, Peter. *Supercars.* Gearhead Garage.
Mankato, MN: Black Rabbit Books, 2017.

Oachs, Emily Rose. *Maserati GranTurismo.* Car Crazy.
Minneapolis: Bellwether Media, Inc., 2018.

WEBSITES

2019 Maserati GranTurismo
**www.maseratiusa.com/maserati/us/en/models/
granturismo**

Maserati GranTurismo
www.caranddriver.com/maserati/granturismo

INDEX

B

body design, 10,
   12–13, 14

C

colors, 18

costs, 27

D

driving modes, 23

E

engines, 4, 7, 10, 14,
   20, 22, 23

H

history, 7, 8–9

I

interior design, 17, 18, 26

S

speeds, 4, 20, 21

suspension, 24